Not a Violin

Not a Violin

Poems by

Martin Agee

© 2025 Martin Agee. All rights reserved.
This material may not be reproduced in any form, published,
reprinted, recorded, performed, broadcast,
rewritten or redistributed without
the explicit permission of Martin Agee.
All such actions are strictly prohibited by law.

Cover design by Shay Culligan
Cover image by Chidy Young on Unsplash
Author photo by Matt Dine

ISBN: 978-1-63980-853-3
Library of Congress Control Number: 2026931554

Kelsay Books
502 South 1040 East, A-119
American Fork, Utah 84003
Kelsaybooks.com

For Tamara

Martin Agee's *Not a Violin,* nullifies, initially, the idea of being a violin, of music. What a violin is—a God, a human, a life, a space in between—is everywhere in this collection.

The poems are all music and so, in this sense, the book is its own kind of instrument. It's an instrument of desire and truth with a consistency of presence. There is always something there, watching, lurking, that has both bigness and smallness to it. He writes, "Some nights a very large dog sits at the foot of my bed/growling . . ." The growl is everywhere in this book, and it is a song, that big dog, too.

Agee's gift is the gift of surprise and reflection. One never feels comfortable in these poems, like you know where it will take you, and this is the joy. This is the sonic and visual landscape of *Not a Violin.* When you put it down you will still hear its notes in your daily doings. Listen!

—Matthew Lippman, author of *We Are All Sleeping with Our Sneakers On*

Acknowledgments

Thank you to the following publications, in which versions of these poems previously appeared:

Book of Matches: "There Are a Few of Us for Whom *Scheherazade* Brings Back Those Nights, Not the Arabian Ones, When We Smoked Cheap Cigars in a Jungle Gym Spaceship"

Jerry Jazz Musician: "The Köln Concert," "Frank Zappa Presents Edgard Varèse"

Parcham: "Eucalyptus Soliloquy"

Willows Wept Review: "Sometimes at the Café There Are Warblers"

The author also wishes to thank:

Matthew Lippman, without whom this collection would not exist. Joel Agee, Marcia Butler, Judy Freni, Doris Keesling, Carl Powers, David Powers, Tamara Powers, Theodore Powers, Rebecca Pyle, Effi Shaked, Christine (C.J.) Trotter,

and Belinda Whitney, for believing.

Contents

Part 1

Prayer Near the Villa Borghese	19
The Köln Concert	20
Eucalyptus Soliloquy	22
Shiny Silver Buttons	24
Shaving Cream on Tulips	27
There Are a Few of Us for Whom *Scheherazade* Brings Back Those Nights, Not the Arabian Ones, When We Smoked Cheap Cigars in a Jungle Gym Spaceship	30
The Grace of the Mop and Bucket	32
Search for a New Land	34
Arrived New York	36
Spiked	38
Frank Zappa Presents Edgard Varèse	40
Even the Dog Doesn't Hear	41
Taking Time Out from Practicing to Eat Everything in Sight	44

Part 2

In Solitary	49
Where Shadows Go	51
Sometimes There Are Bears II	53
Burnt Toast	56
Sometimes at the Café There Are Warblers	58
How I Wish I Had Known the Names	60
Ascolta i Bambini	61
ICE 648 Innsbruck	62

Ninety-Six Harleys   65
Searching for Doris After Sunset   67

Part 3

Red Hair   71
Upon Seeing a Google Earth Image of Where I Live   73
Total Eclipse   75
Inside the Case   77
Requiem   78
Gifts   79
Lovers of the Ocean   82
Poem Without Any Sentimental Lines in It   84
Adagio for Strings   86
Beethoven Nine   89
A Few Seconds of Joy   90
I've Played a Lot of Broadway Shows in My Life, Some of Them Huge Hits with Names Like *Crazy for You, Fiddler on the Roof, Merrily We Roll Along* (Once a Huge Flop, Later a Huge Hit), and of Course the Ones That Never Should Have Been Done in the First Place: *Carrie, Lestat, A Tale of Two Cities,*   91
Broadway Chocolate Pushers   94
I Am Not a Violin   96

*Dedicated to the memory
of Debbie Bernfeld*

Part 1

Prayer Near the Villa Borghese

On still nights when the concert halls are dark, I can hear tuxedos weeping in their closets. They long to be worn again but fear that last night's concert may have been their last. And so, they are having a cry. Some are torn from overuse. Others are stained by the salt, the sweat of the violinist, the oboist, the conductor, after a thousand nights in warm-up rooms and under spotlights. Some are white; like sad ghosts they hang in closets and wait alongside forgotten Halloween costumes and the gown a bridesmaid wore only once. Some of them know they will never be worn again by the conductor who lost his balance and tumbled into the orchestra pit of obscurity, or the violinist who lost his hearing.

Who knows in what closet Brahms's last white tie and tails coat hangs, weeping? Maybe it's in a landfill with Mozart's despairing powdered wig. Toscanini's white gloves and Elvis's blue suede shoes are there too, heartbroken.

Outside my window near the Villa Borghese, the stone pines are speaking to me. They are asking me to pray for joy. And so I pray for the sad tuxedos and weeping tails coats—that their tears are not tears of grieving but tears of jubilation. I pray that after their last concert they will light up the sky and ride upon flames into the arms of waiting children that will dream forth and fill all their future concert halls with elation, with eternal melody, with rejoicing, with the Pines of Rome.

The Köln Concert

I'm listening to the Köln Concert
and it is déjà vu. It's Keith Jarrett playing
the music I always knew but never listened to.
It is every night at midnight putting away the violin
and sitting alone somewhere on the Kansas prairie
playing the piano. I play and play, and it is a search.
It is like praying and searching.
A search for something to put the tears in. A receptacle
for tears. All of them: my mother's tears, my father's tears.
My brother's tears. All the tears of the world spilling
onto the ivory keys making them slick, slippery,
fingers sliding across the surface of my alone hours
at midnight when no one listens, no one cares,
no faces peer at me through windows
the way they did when I practiced Tchaikovsky
and imitation Paganini caprices, every note tortured
and out of tune. I should have been a painter
or a fisherman in Colorado. I miss the mountains
smiling at me like they used to
in the windswept valley of sagebrush and lone pine,
antelope rushing next to the car window,
the Snowy Range in the windshield clear
as mother of pearl, the cat's eye shooter
that I still carry in my pocket for luck

and reminding me of those sunny days in the west
where my footprints still mark the dusty roads
and my legs are fenceposts that anchor my weight
deep into the soil of home and lean
into the wind, the wind that dries the sweat
that falls on the keyboard and wide-grained spruce
stained permanent with salt that mixes with tears,
the fingers fast and slick on the ivories, no science,
no lessons, no juries, no jealous lovers,
no mother pointing a finger. It's midnight now,
no, it's two a.m. but it doesn't matter, I'm staying the night
till the concert is ended and there's nothing left,
no mountains, no fenceposts.

Eucalyptus Soliloquy

The pavements of my youth
were never paved at all, really—
gravel, loose along the edges,
a dialogue

between distant Eucalyptus groves
and self-built landscapes of borrowed trees,
orphaned leaves and fallen limbs
along the side of the road.

Half a world away
the termites went about their work
hollowing logs
as I trembled near a steep embankment.

Barbed wire fences, invisible at dusk—
kept cattle off the road
but threatened the tender flesh
of inner arms,

easily scarred
like the boy I wish I knew
who turned and walked away
with a bottle of rose wine in one hand

and a violin in the other.
Standing atop a mountain pass,
the droning didgeridoo is barely audible
and the wait is long

for a hummingbird
that slipped off the side of the road
just beyond the bend
and tumbled into the valley.

Shiny Silver Buttons

When I was five I got my first Kodak instamatic.
A brown plastic box easy to hold with awkward hands,
a tiny window to squint through with one eye closed tight.

Dad said point it toward the pasture and press down
on the shiny silver button to catch the horses.
But I was clumsy and ended up

taking a picture of my knees and my sister's hula hoop
in the driveway. My masterpiece

was of the neighbor's cat crossing the street in front of our house.
A calico I think, but so far away—
a dark smudge on asphalt

and maybe it wasn't a cat after all, it might have been
my brother's baseball glove. The first time I saw the ocean,
I pressed the shiny silver button and ten days later

Dad drove me to Walgreens. I picked up an envelope full
of black and whites, most of them grainy,
one with ten percent ocean at the bottom,

ninety percent sky at the top, and a closeup of
my left index finger
that strayed in front of the lens.

In college I took photography as an elective.
The first permanent photograph in history was taken
in 1826 in Le Gras by the inventor Nicéphore Niépce.

There was no silver button to push—he used a camera
obscura to project a scene from out his window
onto bitumen for eight hours, an eternity

during which Mendelssohn penned the last twenty-four bars
of the Overture to A Midsummer Night's Dream,
and an unknown sailor fell overboard and drowned

on the maiden voyage of the HMS Beagle. You can't see
Mendelssohn or a sailing ship in that photo

but they are there.
You can see them inside sunlight
bouncing off rooftops and the vineyards of a French countryside.

You can see the mother who labored in childbirth
for eight hours, only to die
and leave behind an orphan

who invented Riemannian manifolds
and number theory.
You can see a nameless artisan in Kyoto

whose daughter fell from a horse
as he carved woodblock prints of ducks and caterpillars.
They are there, all of them frozen

in bitumen. In my closet there's an SLR.
It's a black box with a screen on the back—
you push down on the shiny silver button

and something inside clicks, a shutter
opens and closes
in a fraction of a second.

Once I used it to take a snapshot
of my eight-year-old learning to ride a bike, smiling, proud.

The shutter speed was set to $1/1000^{th}$ of a second,
an eternity during which
the entire universe froze

as my daughter peddled furiously to stay upright.
If you narrow your eyes just a bit,
in that photo you will see:

a girl searching for roly-polies in a rock garden,
a boy with clumsy hands pressing shiny silver buttons—

pounding the piano keys,
cursing the fingerboard—

an Emperor penguin
slipping on the ice in Antarctica,

and a mother in Kansas singing Edelweiss
as she rocks her newborn to sleep, his heavy eyes
dreaming inside sunlight.

Shaving Cream on Tulips

Some nights a very large dog sits at the foot of my bed,
growling. I am the duck in Peter and the Wolf

and Karloff is the narrator. The light seeps like lava,
so hot it burns. A hand reaches for me, brandishing

a hot iron half an inch from my throat.
It's always about the throat.

I open the milk carton from the wrong end and wait
torturous hours

for my overdone steak. *Come back home* says a voice,
but the house has burned to the ground,

my stamp collection, the cat, the emerald and turquoise
carpet all covered with vomit, the green chandelier

shattered in patterns of math
music on the ceiling. The white brick,

not white anymore.
There's shaving cream on the tulips,

raw eggs drip from my father's knees. A lamp explodes
as I fall backward on the sofa

listening to Bolero over and over, the soprano sax
of a garden, a secret garden

where boys play with matches and undress
behind olive trees. They kick each other in the shins

until their throats hurt.
Shards of glass in my hair, a flood

in the basement. The water from below,
fire from above. Bedroom door cracked

and I peer out to see if the world is still there.
My best friend's mother is driving down the hall.

She pulls into Exxon instead of Mobil,
and from the back seat I ask

why are we stopping here.
She looks in the rear-view mirror

and says *this is where we get gas for ski trips*
but I can't even make it up the rope tow

so I reach for a violin
and drink whiskey with equestrians. The dog shows its teeth

and I lie awake searching for the right notes,
the wild horses at the bottom of the ocean.

There Are a Few of Us for Whom *Scheherazade* Brings Back Those Nights, Not the Arabian Ones, When We Smoked Cheap Cigars in a Jungle Gym Spaceship

on a playground, where the little kids climbed to the top and sang the chorus of *Hey Jude* over and over at recess. It's the last week of school, and blue smoke rises—no, circles into the night sky and you are face to face with the lone trumpet days of summer. Sprinklers are running

in the back yard. You lie upon the wet ground and listen to the intermittent thump-thumping of skateboards as they roll and hiss along sections of sidewalk pink from old chalk drawings and bloodied knees. The sound of the orchestra and the scent of just cut grass

are wrapped together, melded, and stored on the shelf. You blink and you're sitting in the balcony of Carnegie Hall the night after your father's heart stopped. Déjà vu: you close your eyes, and the cello solo is pulling you back to the living room,

those warm evenings with the black and white TV. Lenny is explaining families of instruments as the aroma of Mom's pot pies comes out of the oven and the sound of Elvis's guitar comes out of your sister's room. Those pot pies! The mac and cheese ones. The smell of them grabs you like the solo flute of the Prince's Theme, and every time you hear it for the rest of your life, you'll think about Dad reading *The History of Mankind* and Mom in the basement watching Johnny Carson. The aroma of sound. The pot pies baking in the oven. The same

rusted oven that sits like an abandoned child atop a landfill, whispering stories to the seagulls of families that weren't so lucky. Their oldest son came home from war in a flag draped coffin, and never, never will the smell of cheap cigars,

nor the screaming of the trumpet, nor the thumping of skateboards, nor Elvis, nor the Beatles, ever bring him back. His unborn children will never remember their mother's embrace upon hearing the solo oboe,

but her lily of the valley scent will remain long after the horses in the pasture have turned to dust and the land is cracked, barren amid echoes of violins and cellos telling tales of The Arabian Nights.

The Grace of the Mop and Bucket

It is the duty of every artist,
and musician, to tell the story of the custodian.
Summoned to the classroom of *a horse*
my kingdom for a horse with mop and bucket,
he wipes the vomit
from under the desk of a girl we made fun of
when she asked
about warm lips and *holy palmers' kiss.*

Where is the bronze statue
of the janitor who smiled as he swept the hallways
after school? When I asked him for help with history
he replied: *the girl, she's always right here . . .* gnarled hand
over his chest
next to an embroidered name no one remembers.
He polished the gymnasium floor

and scrubbed the urinals, whistling the Prince's Theme
from *Scheherazade* all the while.
Who will compose a symphony
for the man who climbed ladders with a hundred and one keys
    jingling on his belt
as he replaced fluorescent lights flickering
in the conference rooms of Senators
and chemistry labs? Look

for an empty shelf of poetry
about a janitor for whom the Chevy Station Wagon
is home. He's been swept away

and lies among
broken concrete and twisted iron
that washed down Main Street years ago. Tears
ran down his mother's face

when he sang a solo at Sunday school and played
the part of Tybalt in fifth grade. He was stabbed
on a playground of addiction
before reaching high school. They found him on a bus
headed toward abandoned
warehouses of amusement parks after his father
shot himself with a pistol.

At the Art Institute, the man with a top hat frowns
and waits for a figure in uniform
to pull weeds and cut the grass on *A Sunday Afternoon
at La Grande Jatte.* The woman—the one with a parasol—turns
    away
as Gaga sings *baby, you were born this way*
and the groundskeeper smiles,
humming in the rain.

Search for a New Land

I wrote my future while the world watched TV
and went to drive-in movies. Seinfeld and Saturday
Night Fever were verbs in hibernation, passing days
were drawers full of blank stationary and unused
postage stamps. My postcards to tomorrow lived
on a fingerboard covered with sweat as the leaves
fell. Out of tune, a bleating newborn lamb standing
upon wobbly legs in the pasture gradually gave way
to birdsong worthy of pastorales and inheritances.
Agile fingers mastered the science of placement
and vibrato, and a purple iris made its first appearance
in the snow.

But I discovered the future is not just earned—
it's inherited too. And the silence between the notes
was my inheritance: breathing and quietude gave way
to forests of anxiety. Somewhere in a far-off city
a savant was taking the stage as I languished
on the prairie.

The accelerating future met the slowing past,
colliding on the runways of the internet
before screens were carried in pockets.
No Google matches, no Facebook likes, no YouTube views.
No TikTok.
Mozart buried in a pauper's grave of monetization,
Brahms in a silicon cloud.

Shakespeare didn't tweet.

What is worthy of inheritance? I have searched the horizon,
and though it is always far, there is a new land
of bountiful sunflowers where past is future,
and Mozart symphonies are remembered.
A future of oratorios written in the key of empathy
and harmonies that tell the stories of ebony
and flaxen clouds, their richness,
their unity.

Arrived New York

After Ray Gonzalez

Everything was a snow day and a mother's damp apron.
The endless back yard, miniature racing cars, monarch butterflies,
single-engine airplanes dropping chocolates out of the sky
to get rid of the thistles. This is how bees sting
opened fingers. Bare feet have no steel plates built into their soles;
the next brick of the clock tower is laid.

Green carpeting no longer absorbs spilled milk.
Hardwood collects ash that's pushed around my walk-up studio.
A novelist whose heart stopped in a taxicab
rises out of eighty-four years of death to cheer.
Cambered maple from far away
lies in wait to become a violin.

It's all about the rain and the guy in a dark alley.
A broken piano on a street corner.
A guy named Arkady points out a woman wearing a scarf and
    Prada—
it's Barbra Streisand.
Real men wear hardhats and operate jackhammers with gunshot
    mufflers.
The lead pipe is always held aloft in a subway car.

Rubbing the bare shoulder of a girl from Malaysia with my bare
    foot.
Sushi is amazing but there's mercury in tuna.
What happened to the guy I saw last week
dragging an open crate full of toilet seats and fish
through Grand Central?

What happened to checker cabs?
What it means to wear a yarmulke.
Down the block there is a schoolyard in the middle of the street.
First hashish ever. Finding a time-capsule
with a disintegrating crucifix that wishes it was something else.
My back yard is a rusted fire escape.
The violin is stuffed with cotton that fell from a tree

outside
my long-ago window.
I can still smell the freshly cut grass,
the lilac bush,
the trains,
antique steam engines,
the mountains,
parking lots,
pitchers of beer,
alfalfa fields,
Christmas trees,
snakes with venom.

Children fly through tunnels that were hidden
under the dirt floors of their prairie homesteads.
Some of them live on my fire escape, tapping at the window.

Every day they help me lay bricks and achieve
a better bow grip: they know first-hand
the ambitions of caterpillars.

Spiked

I'm riding the subway to work one night
and when we get to Columbus Circle
a woman with spiked orange hair and purple lips
walks into the car with her son, maybe five or six years old.
They sit down across from me; she reaches in his backpack
and takes out a book: *Katie's Family*.
The picture on the cover shows a girl standing between two men—
    she's holding their hands.

Well, this mother starts reading to her son:
Katie's school is having a Mother's Day celebration,
but Katie doesn't have a mother.
So she brings her two fathers with her to class
and she's a little nervous—
but her two dads are in love and know what it means
to be a family.
I'm watching this mother, reading to her boy

about Katie on the subway,
and I can't help wishing
I'd had a mother like that—
not the one sitting on the sofa
reaching for Almond Joys
and cans of SlimFast laced with vodka
at eleven in the morning.

The boy reaches up and touches his mom's orange hair,
and I'm reading the graffiti on the seat next to them:
an encyclopedia
of spray-painted stories—
like how a boy's mother embarrassed her son
in front of a shoe salesman
while his father was shooting heroin in the alleyway.
What if my mother had spiked hair? Would that have made me
a better father?
Would I have put my arm around my own daughter
on the subway and read to her
about Katie's family, or
taken her to the Stonewall and explained to her
what happened there in 1969? Maybe
I wouldn't have had to spend the rest of my life regretting
that I didn't take her to that Metallica concert when she was
    sixteen—

because I'll never know
if she loved thrash guitar or wanted piercings and a tattoo.

Frank Zappa Presents Edgard Varèse

Based on actual events

In the winter of 1981 we were hired to play Downtown—
a performance in Greenwich Village billed "Frank Zappa Presents:
a Musical Tribute to Edgard Varèse." I sat on stage,
wearing black, tuning my violin, warming up,
looking out at the audience milling around, most of them
covered in tattoos and piercings of every body part
waiting for Frank to take the stage while the smell of weed
wafted through the hall from somewhere in the back. Frank
was nowhere to be seen, but we started playing *Offrandes:*
avant-garde music for Soprano and Chamber Orchestra
that Varèse wrote in 1921. Some think it sounds less like music
and more like noise, and our audience wasn't having it.

They were there to see Frank on stage belting out
Who are the Brain Police or some other Mothers
of Invention tune and what was this classical bullshit
we were playing? Three minutes in, the smell of pot
getting thicker, they started—boos, catcalls, heckling,
bellowing: *Frank! we want Frank!*
Well, out walks Frank in a black tuxedo and the crowd goes nuts.
He cuts us off right in the middle of it and turns to them,
yelling back: *You're all a bunch of fucking assholes!*

No Varèse, no jazz; no jazz, no Elvis; no Elvis, no Dylan;
no Dylan, no Beatles: none of us would be here without them.
No Beatles, no Frank Zappa; no Zappa, no Mothers of Invention:
you jerks wouldn't have nothin' to listen to but church hymns—
sit your loser butts down and listen to some real music
with the same reverence you'd pay your own mother
for the day she labored to give birth to your sorry ass!

Even the Dog Doesn't Hear

I'm uptown
standing on 103rd Street
when it occurs to me how big New York City is,
and for some reason I'm feeling small.
There's a man smoking outside the Chinese kitchen on Broadway,
    all dressed in white
with a dirty apron
and he's maybe the tallest dude I've ever seen; I mean,
this guy should be playing center for the Knicks,
not washing dishes.
Then there's this giant walking toward me from across the street,
    all in black,
with a fur hat and payos,
towering over me as he reaches the curb. The ground shakes;
he's the Paul Bunyon
of Hasidim.
A jogger
is coming and I duck behind a fire hydrant just in time
to avoid being squashed under her running shoe.
I'm a lanternfly, one those pests
with wings spotted red and blue. No, even smaller—I'm a ladybug
that identifies as a man.
I yell up at the jogger *Hey, watch where you're going!*
but she doesn't hear.
No one does.
There's a guy walking a dog up the street and I scramble
to get as far away from the hydrant as I can, but this dog,
it's like a new breed of Humongous Great Dane. No, bigger
even than that, it's the constellation Canis Major—

I've never seen a dog this big.
I yell up at the owner *Hey, what kind of dog is that?*
but he ignores me—even the dog
doesn't hear
and I'm getting smaller and smaller.
A woman walks by in shiny red heels, her legs bigger than Kansas
tornados. Everything is a gigantic funnel cloud
and everyone
is walking fast. I guess
they are in a hurry to escape,
people in New York City usually are, but I think to myself
this could be bad so I start yelling at the top of my lungs
somebody help me!
but they can't
or don't hear, and the louder I scream, the bigger everything
    around me gets.
Soon I can't tell if there are people anymore, it's just
gigantic boulders crashing down
on the sidewalk all around me. Mount St. Helens has erupted
right here on Manhattan Island.
I think about dodging off the curb into the street, but there's no
    way the drivers
are going to see me and taxis never slow down in New York,
even for baby strollers or Ronald McDonald balloons
so why would they hit the brakes to save me?
Over here!
I scream but no one hears.

There's a puddle left over from this morning's rain
and I've fallen in—it's the Pacific Ocean—I'm an amoeba
swimming the Big Apple and
no one can hear me,
or see me,
except under an electron microscope the size of skyscrapers.
This must be an Isaac Asimov novel, or one of those sci-fi B-
    movies from 1957,
The Incredible Shrinking Man or *Attack of the 50 Ft. Woman* and
    now
I've entered a black hole and re-materialized as
a mountain climber or a Christian
or a heart surgeon or a plumber or a Jew or a Sikh
or a violinist on 103rd street, my open case littered with change.

Taking Time Out from Practicing to Eat Everything in Sight

In memory of Raphael Bronstein

Practicing the violin has produced nothing but frustration for me as of late. I've been struggling with playing softly, and there's a piece I'm performing next week that has a lot of *pianissimo* passages. I'm not talking about the *pppppp* of Tchaikovsky's Pathétique symphony—this music is softer even than that. The marking in the score is *pianissimo possibile* (as soft as possible).

I start my day practicing before breakfast with an hour of scales as soft as I can play, but get nowhere. So I decide to take a break, and I glance at my to-dos for the day. Decluttering is at the top of the list. Everything must go. I start in the kitchen, but it dawns on me I didn't have breakfast and I'm ravenous. I'm in no mood for food prep, so I check the fridge for something quick and easy. The vegetable drawer is full, and I take out some yams and potatoes. *What the hell,* I say out loud as I begin devouring them raw. Next I reach for the onions and garlic. There's no real need to peel or sauté them. I move on to the meat: a few hot dogs are left (they are just fine uncooked) and I finish the pastrami sandwich left over from yesterday's lunch as well. On the bottom shelf there are turkey burgers; I still have plenty of room for those. The milk is approaching expiration, so I drink it right out of the container and, once the carton's empty, take a few bites of that too. Milk cartons are surprisingly good.

Back in my office I pick up the violin, and for some reason at that very moment I think about my violin teacher, Mr. Bronstein. A memory, like mist. No, more than that—it's as if he's speaking to me in quiet tones with his thick Russian accent. Something about soft playing . . . only I can't remember.

I brush the memory aside and continue with etudes, but I'm not improving. Still hungry, I decide to resume decluttering, starting with the closets. My old collection of CDs must go, but rather than tossing them I munch on them. A box of used guitar strings looks tempting. I've been meaning to clear out all those books I never bothered to read, and what better way to dispose of *Crime and Punishment* than to simply eat it, dust jacket and all? I consume both *The Iliad* and *1984* in one gulp and have Shakespeare for dessert.

*

Violin in hand, I ponder Mr. Bronstein again, and it's much clearer now—he's right here in the room with me. I recall his explanation of getting softer, of *diminuendo,* at one of my violin lessons long ago. I was in New York, at his apartment on 101st Street, true story, and he was at the piano describing *diminuendo al niente* (decreasing to nothing). He played the same note, a b-flat, over and over maybe eight or ten times in succession, but every single one of them was much softer than the one before. And as I stood in front of him watching, Mr. Bronstein's entire body was changing, morphing. He was getting stronger, no, heavier . . . it was as if he was gaining weight with each note he played. At the same time, the sound of the b-flat was getting lighter and softer and lighter still, until at last it evaporated into nothing. Bronstein was getting bigger, denser, heavier than any man I've ever seen, until finally, in real time, he had become a behemoth. More than a behemoth.

The entire universe was inside of him, down inside his throat, and the proof was there for all to see: he could play *pianissimo diminuendo al niente* with the body of a blue whale and the touch of a butterfly on mint.

Part 2

In Solitary

Those were the years I spent the hours pacing
while the moon and shoe salesmen roamed free. I paced
the floor—paced and paced. Three paces up. A window

covered in moss . . . no light.
Three paces back. A heavy iron door,
elephants and sad clowns just beyond.

Through an opening a hand
provided oranges and not enough licorice.
Wastewater

flowed from the street above, carrying discarded crusts
of sheet music and lace curtains.
I paced. Two paces right. A chain,

pounded into the wall
by a woman holding a tin flute in one hand
and a broken whiskey bottle in the other. Blood

dripped green on the floor. Two paces left. A rusted cot
where I slept, covered in frothy milk and potato skins. Overhead,
circles of light

where cockroaches hid behind the beams. Leaves fell,
arranging themselves neatly into a pile in the corner:
the brotherhood of raking, forbidden. A grey horse

behind a fence—paced, searched
for blades of grass, and waited
for a flat-bed wagon pulled by mules with blinders.

I pace. Pace and pace—ten paces the perimeter,
cinderblocks struggle to get even
with lavender and thyme.

I pace and pace. A few feet away
thistles and dandelions defeat the roses and choke the sun
at midnight.

Where Shadows Go

Always nearby, my shadow is longer than the Nile
and sadder than Robin Williams.
The shadows of lampposts and skyscrapers, weary
and sad. They want it to be nighttime; turn off the day.

Sometimes when the sun is about to roll off a mountain,
I put on Ray-Bans and stop to ask my shadow:
How are you feeling? He never answers—
my caller-ID shows unknown or I'm spam. I text

a friend: *How are you feeling?* but she's in the hospital.
Something inside of her broke.
Her fingers are too weak to text or rub
a puppy's ears. After sundown I visit her and mouth words,
    worthless

like *you look okay,* because I never understood how to protect
an abandoned kitten, or a mother when the casualty officer
walked a driveway to ring the doorbell, or a life friend
with a diagnosis and no way out.

Where do shadows go
to get happy after being long and sad all day? Some
may jump off bridges.
Others, I imagine they climb trees and play

amongst racoons and redstarts. The shadow of a dog
frolics on a beach as Mary Travers croons
and a foal lies on wet grass
in the shadow of a stone pine that danced all night

in the eternal city. Came the cell towers,
casting their shadows and promises
to find the last digit of pi
as if that was going to make great pizza

and wine. One night after dark, I walked
near a pub, a loud commotion heard from within. I peered
through frosted glass and saw all the shadows of the world
laughing their asses off till dawn.

Sometimes There Are Bears II

After Randon Billings Noble

Two bears
in the kitchen, the door left ajar.
One in the closet
trying on my black tie.
How will I
get dressed for work? He will
rush at me, pouncing.
He always does.

It may happen during a concert
or a ballet. A recital.
Even a play—Lear
may be on the program,
but I know no Shakespeare.
My breath shallow,
my mouth dry, I've forgotten the Preludio—
there are no Bach inventions,
no Mozart symphonies.
I can't find the notes,
my hands
shaking con artists
on a fingerboard. Dread
has taken a seat behind me,

panic is my stand partner
the bear
with claws like razors, rears up
and growls.
He always does.

On the other side of the footlights,
high up in the balcony
a bear
speaks to strangers.
He is down there with a violin, he says.
*I've been following him
on his journey.* Above him,
above the ceiling,
bears, older than Sophocles,
older than the pyramids,
are circling the sky.

To the west, just above the horizon,
a brave hunter
keeps watch. His hand reaches down,
touches my shoulder.
He whispers:
Sometimes there are bears.

Be kind to them.
Welcome them
into your kitchen, your closet.
Keep them
in your violin case. Invite them
to follow you to the stage door
and onto airplanes.
They will live in you, they will guide you,
always. Without them

you are lost
in a starless night.

Burnt Toast

Every day I drink from a porcelain cup
filled with shadows.

I drink the shadow of a foal
in the pasture and dance
on a carpet of wet field grass
while men roll dice
under a bridge. I wonder, if that foal
survives, will it roam free
on the dunes or will it be carted off
to pull heavy artillery. Or will it become
the sturdy horse my grandfather rode on the farm.

Even white horses cast shadows
until they are swallowed.

Cellos grew in a forest once,
before it was razed
to make room for cloud server farms.
Dead trees keep casting their shadows
until the porcelain cup is empty.

I drink the shadow of a tangled mass
of electrical wires. It appears
on the wall behind my desk
at three in the morning; my skin

slips out from the bedsheets. It crawls
on the ceiling and hangs dry
while my entrails lie there, awake
in the shadows of electrons
that mix with saliva
and explode the blood.

In the morning, I leave the porcelain cup
on the table and step outside
to drink the shadow of the moon as it passes
in front of the sun, but in the kitchen
burnt toast comes out of the toaster—black,
the smell of it never goes away.

Sometimes at the Café There Are Warblers

Out my window there's a village
built of cardboard and broken plastic,

and there's a trampoline there too. You start jumping,
higher and higher you jump and soon you're over the wall,

over a cloud or inside a rainbow
looking down on the brownish canopy of a forest

that's starving.
In school I was taught

forests never need to be fed; they have all they need.
But that teacher grew old and died like any other

and I was left wondering, afraid. That fires or a meteorite
or pine beetles were going to be the end of them one day,

and it would be my fault
because I didn't shout out to the trees and give them

love. That's what they needed to be fed.
That's what they need. Huge quantities

of love. And sonnets, symphonies. Maybe
a baseball card or two. But mostly

love. And all the many trees,
the ash, the sandalwood,

eucalyptus and sheesham that consume the love
will make more love. Lots of it.

And they will sing about love. Not the Greenpeace kind,
the sweaty kind

with throbbing trunks and orgasmic
bending of branches

inward and out,
forward and back, rhythmic, wild, their roots

curling in ecstasy. Sometimes
at the café there are warblers

singing in the rafters
but no one hears.

I order the kale and oats
brought out on broken plastic trays,

but a girl at the next table
is jumping on a trampoline.

Higher and higher she jumps, until she can hear
the vibrations of warblers as they sing

the same songs
sung by spruce, curly maple, and whales.

How I Wish I Had Known the Names

of the sculptors living in nursing homes
where I played the Preludio with my eyes closed
so I wouldn't see the open sores, the blood-soaked bandages
torn off in a hell of no sleep and traffic jams
of wheelchairs in the hallways
mowed down by white jackets and mops,
buckets carried by volunteers—they used to call them candy
    stripers,
which sounded good, then
come to realize the red stripes on their uniforms
were the lyrics of *I Want to Hold Your Hand* in blood.

My candy striping career consisted
of holding a violin with sweaty palms,
playing sonatas and partitas
as the smells of rosin and marble dust evaporated,
time slipped away in an ashen pall, and never
no, never did I learn their names:
the painters, plumbers, the schoolteachers,
the grandmothers
who served up figs and ice cream by day
and clawed at bandages by night.

Ascolta i Bambini

Listen to children. They are speaking to you. With smooth bare feet they steal away across white sand beaches like glide planes above a mist, romping with ponies and goldens by the sea and building caves of queens and kingfishers. Children fly.

Ascolta i bambini. With laughter they swim near the moray eels and barracudas of the lake. Swings carry them out, keeping them safe, above riffles and diamonds that hide the unseeable. Children go toward the danger. Always, they are speaking to you.

Ascolta i bambini. They are speaking to you even in their sleep with dreamcatchers upon a thousand moons and test flights over sandcastles. They hover above the mint and clover of carousel horses and sail in boats that have no sails. Children choose the land of ginger and gemstones.

Ascolta i bambini. They are speaking in music. They understand the *Adagio, Allegro,* the *Andantino.* Clowns sing the *Lamento* and dragons whistle the *Melodia,* and children do the translating. Sunlight through the window casts spirals and rainbows across cave walls and the ceiling moves in the harmonization of melodies and mobiles. Children feel the *Allargando.*

I bambini ascolteranno. Children will listen. They are always listening. They hear the villanelles, the idylls of woodwinds, the warnings of the tympani. The lying of parents and the rantings of statesmen, the firing of cannons—the syllogism is complete, the dreamcatchers will fall.

Ascolta i bambini.

ICE 648 Innsbruck

You barely notice when it starts moving
and for a moment
you glance out the window as the platform
begins to slide away, a waving stranger
you wish you had known
or gotten to know
but you feel nothing
as it starts to gather speed.
A warmth inside you, a butterfly
stretching its wings as it holds on
to the chrysalis a split second longer
before letting go
and flitting
flying
sliding

into a blue pasture of sunlight and sun
flowers of every shade known to butterflies
but not us. The way
you look at them, all the many strangers,
wishing every footstep of their life
had brought them closer to you,
your arms,
lips closer and feeling the touch, the breath, the breast,
the heat
of another human who breathes
the same air, sings the same songs, plays the same music,
tells the same tales for a thousand
and seven thousand years

of being alone, oh
the loneliness inside a chrysalis
that pulses and bursts
upon white sand beaches and walks barefoot amongst
moist clover—

hears the church bell ring at sunrise and listens
to the hum
the thrum of the city
beneath worn feet that long to flee,
to fly as butter
flies as a butterfly
hesitating
not ever hesitating to take the leap
to fly into the blue mountain spring
that washes over us down
every throat singing
the world is down there
and the butterflies and the birds of the world are all down there
joining the celebration
the train leaves the station
and heads into a great countryside
where lonely sheep wear bells around their necks—
heard from pastures at great distances
behind hills, mountains,
lakes that pulse with light and shadow,
all seen
unseen.

How I wish
I wish I had known
every one of them
the men, the women, the children that I
left behind there on the platform waving, their hidden streams,
their flowing hair with aroma of honey,
their worn shoes
that carried them a thousand miles. But
there were rivers of my own to cross, maths to solve, landscapes
to paint, scales to master, harmonies to invent
notes to learn, the concertinos
of butterflies, the etudes of flowers, the science
of Newton and Mozart
and before I blinked
the snow was falling and my legs hurt
but the world
down inside me was warm, sliding silently
by the window
and I could at long last feel
I was moving
faster than light.

Ninety-Six Harleys

hammer the pavement at 124 decibels
which I'm told is louder than someone screaming
in your ear
they thunder down the block
a quarter to midnight
hotter than the Flaming Mountains
but the A.C. is on and everyone is sleeping
shotgun mufflers over their ears
AR-15s under their pillows
the rumble
the glare of billion
candle per square inch headlights
targeting kelp forests and icecaps
the bottom of a warm ocean even
where everyone hides for cover
the coral reef above them
dying
dual exhaust pipes spit out killer phantoms
that hang over beaches and parks
the stench overpowering
the sickening gangrene
of flesh torn by war
and school shootings
the rotting bark of ancient trees
in the Arctic Circle
it's almost midnight
everyone sleeps
with almond scented glue and conspiracy Alexa dreams
fragrant rosebuds of January in their nostrils

I swear to God
dawn will be of the thousand violins
and when the orchestra gets to Mahler
the blind cavefish will abandon their motorcycles
for the ocean

Searching for Doris After Sunset

Dusk has set in over a Kansas prairie
Where in the dim light

Dust rises from the wheels of a Model T Ford
And a meadowlark alights

On a fence post offering its last evening call
Like a black and white photo

In a violin case
I happened upon up in the attic

Sold a hundred years ago to a stranger
Who also searched after sunset for Doris

As she stood right in front of him
Barely hidden among the blades of grass

Trying to explain why the Model T turned left
And the farmer planted beets instead of corn

Part 3

Red Hair

After James Galvin

The sun was setting and all the nightingales of the North Country
were ablaze. With wings trailing fountains of sparks
they flew like wildfire across a continent
in search of the highest mountain and the deepest valley.
Somewhere the aurora borealis was lighting up the sky
but you couldn't see it for the flames.

One bird, the finest ever seen
with remarkable sweetness of voice,
caught my eye. She danced and tricked me
with her flashing tail that made a mockery
of orange clouds. She serenaded every stranger she met—
the Buddhists, the poets and artists—

shining light on their dark and troubled brows.
A soother of stinging eyes, she jazzed the veins
of the healers and caretakers, and Coltraned the blood
of Paralympians who swam the backstroke
with no arms.
Wandering the globe, always one step ahead

of the terminator into night, her voice
echoed the shimmer of her emerald eyes,
keeping watch over the outcast, the sick,
the *other*—all in childlike wonderment.
Then one day I saw she wasn't a nightingale, nor even a bird at all.
There were no feathers, no flashing tail. Her red hair

fell loose on bare shoulders and her body
was a violin on the prairie. With bow in hand,
I started toward her, ever faster. Running now—
I run toward her every day,
but when I finally reach her
I haven't a clue what I'll play.

Upon Seeing a Google Earth Image of Where I Live

I'm throwing away everything I wrote
about walking on cobblestone pavements
and playing in Carnegie Hall.

I play the violin atop a fence post
for old wooden fence posts
near aspen and barbed wire. Where a meadowlark
sings to a mountain columbine
with its arms around prickly pear
and the sky
swallows mother of pearl.

The meadowlark, it spreads its wings
and blinks before flying off
or dying under a sagebrush.

I walk a dusty road
just south of Woods Landing. There's a Chevy wagon
left there by my father,

who slip-slid down an embankment
to walk among peat bogs and willow
near a bedded down fawn.
He whispered his secrets to the wind
and cut agate
in search of patterns.

I lie in a hammock
of swaying hay, eyes half closed.
The sun is bright above,

the opposite of footlights.
There is no darkness or faceless audience beyond;
I don't need Inderal here. My feet are on the ground,
my legs sink into the earth
next to sprawling roots of a lone pine
that shed its needles long ago. They lie on the ground

but are still green. How can that be?
I live on the prickle of a pinecone
thinking about all the notes I've never tasted.

Total Eclipse

It's getting darker and I'm a worm on the sidewalk
waiting for the rain to fall out of a cloudless sky
and turn my freeze-dried carcass
into something a little squishy, a juicy morsel
for the nightingale that has come out
for the three minutes forty-six seconds of totality
to sing and feast on unsuspecting, creeping, slimy
invertebrates like me with no bodies and no limbs and
how do they hear, do worms even have ears?
I have earworms

the string lines of Beethoven
as he turns the moon and earth upside-down
with a few pencil strokes on paper,
horizontal like worms
crawling on a page: some earworms are bassoons
and basses but I'm thinking to myself
Mozart wrote the Jupiter upside-down in his bed
and then raced to get it down
before powdered lime was scattered
and the worms entered.

I'm whistling the theme of the double fugue
and there's a stranger, staring at me
like what an asshole you are you have no idea
he's the guy that found the lost portrait of Charles Dickens in
    Africa,
and stripped away 150 years of grime and varnish to expose
the affair Dickens had—

everyone who has read *Great Expectations*
knows this about him, he was writing *A Tale
of Two Cities* in the daylight
and shagging his wife's sister

in the dark for three and a half minutes of totality. The same
could probably be said of whomever was the first to explain
    eclipses in 450 B.C.
God knows how you pronounce his name or who he was
sleeping with but his mother was the mother
of invention and I'm thinking that must be where Zappa got the
    idea for the name
of the band that played *I'm the Slime*. Frank knew
that Stravinsky had turned the sun upside-down
and now the stranger sits naked on a bench
thinking this guy doesn't know shit about anything
and whistles the Moonlight Sonata.

Inside the Case

My violin has been waiting
inside the case. Like candles
in the closet—scented ones, still
wrapped in tissue. I bought them
one Sunday in the village, thinking
they would look and smell nice burning
on the secretary next to the leather-bound

journal—the one I picked up in Rome.
I told myself it would be a future home
for things left unsaid, the Amalfi pages
like luxurious bedsheets for words:
I want you near me. But not wanting to risk
spilled ink, misspellings or mistakes, I placed it
on the shelf, next to the unlit candles.

My violin still waits
inside the case. It will always be there—
playing from memory in windowless rooms,
orchestra pits and concert halls. I listen
for the echoes, inspired by artisanal spruce
and curly maple that made it possible for me to ask
for forgiveness.

Requiem

On the day,
you stand on four quivering legs and face
the bare corner of the basement,
eyes vacant,
speaking silently to me as you always have.

I bring you outside,
and though you haven't had water in days,
your urine trickles down
and reddens the grass
with your blood.

One last time I place you on the back seat where
you used to sit up, craning your head out the open window,
speeding down a mountain road ears flapping in the wind,
your rich slobber
streaking your splendorous jowls, saturating the leather of the seat.

Once, you sat with me on the sofa at home, forepaws on my lap
and we listened to Mozart's Requiem.
You cocked your head quizzically
as I lifted my hands and coaxed the sopranos
to give more color to their sound.

But today, I can't bear to let you see or hear
my Lacrimosa.

Gifts

I.

The tops of buildings are on fire
and the shadows of lamp posts
are long.
When I was seven
I went barefoot in the dewy grass of summer
before the sun went down.
My sister, ever bright, laughing, taught me:
sunlight is always somewhere,
even when it's cloudy
at midnight.

II.

A friend told me:
you should be kind to yourself, so
I bought a book and gave it
to myself. I finished it in a day

then went outside—there were two skies.
I turned to my lover and asked
which one was real, but she
had already gone. Somewhere a voice was singing:
I read to swim
and listen for echoes.

III.

What it feels like when

you are riding a brand-new bike
on newly paved asphalt.

Once a boy got a Schwinn for Christmas. It was snowing
so he decided to wait
but the snow never melted.

IV.

When the bananas went over-ripe
and the newspaper was left out in the rain,

my friend played the drums
and spread peanut butter on toast.

Outside his window
purple and white crocus bloomed in the dead of winter.

When his daughter came home from college, he smiled
and said *cancer is a gift.*

He died on a Sunday morning
and was buried at the top of a hill.

V.

How happy to

listen to music

as a wind among aspen leaves.

VI.

The hay is stacked
and the stream is low and clear—
mint grows in the valley. I lie upon a sandbar
that will be gone tomorrow
but wavelets are lapping upon polished rocks
and the fish are darting.

Clouds are hard to touch,
but not for mountaintops
and trees.

VII.

Climbing mountains makes me sing out loud and
trees are generous.

Lovers of the Ocean

I.

You swam in the ocean
and surfed the waves, a lover of the sea, arrogant
in your belief that you understood it. You didn't see the warning
    signs
of rip currents. Lying on the beach
with a girl—
she took your hand and placed it

on her breast,
her lips the taste of salt water as she pulled you under.

II.

You may fly or sail across the ocean,
squinting your eyes
from the bow of a ship—the light playing tricks
on your eyes. You crave to know
what's underneath
the blue surface

like being in love
the first time.

III.

It was our first jaunt
at the beach—we walked barefoot
on the sand. White foam
licked our toes.

Little waves deceived us, and we laughed, scrambled
to keep our clothes dry. No one wants to be caught

savoring the first taste of oranges
or a girl's lips in the back seat of the family car.

IV.

Swimming
in molten lava above waves,
watching them crash on the rocks below. They morph and hiss
into steam and white foam—baby's breath
and roses—the lace of a wedding gown
that caresses the cheek. At twenty-eight

I ran a marathon and played Carnegie Hall. Now
I want to marry the ocean.

Poem Without Any Sentimental Lines in It

Running in parks consists largely
of 1) keeping my eyes on the ground,
watching out for uneven cobblestones
and 2) counting steps. There's an app
on my iPhone to help with that part. It has
a big red heart on a white background.
Practicing the violin isn't all that different.
You keep your eyes down as you listen
for uneven rhythms and out of tune notes.
It's scientific: the string vibrates a certain
number of times per second and the placement
of fingers changes the string length to change
pitches that are strung together to form
a musical line, a melody, a symphony. When
I was young I kept a practice log. Every day
I wrote down how many minutes I practiced.
There was no app, no iPhone, so I wrote it down:
I still have the 3 x 5 note cards with the numbers.
Over the years I've played a lot of Broadway shows
and kept track of those, too. How many times
did I play Fiddler on the Roof? The answer
is written down somewhere. Once I counted
the number of notes on each page and added
them all up and then multiplied that number

by the number of times I played the show
and then added up all the many thousands
of shows and concerts and operas and ballets
and string quartets I played over a lifetime in music
and then I figured out I recently played my billionth
note, all the while keeping my eyes down or
on the notes or on the numbers. That's a lot
of notes. So to keep track of them, I'm constructing
my own app that will tell me how many whole steps
I've missed, how many shows I've done, how many
notes I've played, and it's going to have a big heart
that will be alive, beating, rhapsodic,
asking me to stop, to look up,
and to search the eyes
of the woman
next to me.

Adagio for Strings

Barber's Adagio for Strings visited me in my living room last week, and it was an elk. It wasn't whistling or bugling or stamping its hoof the way you'd expect. It just stood there and said *I am the Barber Adagio that Lenny conducted at Tanglewood in 1975.* And then slowly, in slow motion, it shook its antlers and they filled the room, owned the room. These antlers, they weren't six by six points on each side, these were ∞ by ∞.

The first time the Adagio for Strings visited me was the day I turned thirteen, and it was a fine paintbrush. I began painting the earth by numbers, but it spun out of control and the brush became a pie chart. I started riding trains in circles and doing calculus to paint the sky, but the sun became dizzy, the sky scorched, the earth colorless—my math, inaccurate.

The Adagio for Strings visited me the day my daughter graduated from college, and it was a pair of scuba fins. She was crossing the stage in full gear with mask and oxygen cannisters, ready for the fabulous ocean, rubber fins slap-slapping clapping the stage as she got her diploma, and there was an enormous swan floating atop a lake, blue and mirrored and very, very deep.

The Adagio for Strings visited me a hundred and forty-six days after my father died, and it was a paper airplane. I saw it outside the window of a train in Colorado. I mistook it for a great egret (or a lesser one), soaring, diving, bouncing off the top of a treeless mesa, a beam of light in search of quasars where Dad was building a campfire and miniature dollhouses.

One day during the blight I was walking near Mount Sinai Emergency Room, and there was a refrigeration truck parked on the street outside. It was the Adagio for Strings, awaiting the discharges. There was no vaccine yet, and it was snowing. I saw a white kitten in the middle of Amsterdam Avenue, nearly buried, shivering; I picked it up and placed it under my coat as the motor of the truck idled on. The Barber Adagio lasts about eight minutes, but I stood there in the snow for over an hour while the kitten purred.

Barber's Adagio for Strings visited me yesterday, and it was a vinyl album with a photo of my violin on the cover. There was shaving cream on the chinrest. It laid there on my white Formica kitchen table while I sipped cappuccino, and it said *I am the Barber Adagio your father conducted the day you were born.* My grandfather was a conductor on a train, but I never knew my father conducted the Barber Adagio the day I was born. You can't find this Barber Adagio on YouTube because I looked.

It's not online either. I Googled it and there's no record, no recording, no program, no memory, nothing anywhere of the Adagio for Strings conducted by my father. Nor is there a trace of the one conducted by Ormandy with the Philadelphia Orchestra in 1970, but that one was there too, and it was dew on a blade of grass. It rested there on my white Formica kitchen table, and said *I am the Barber Adagio that Ormandy conducted in 1970.*

I rummaged, looking for the one I played in 1981, the string quartet version. It was there too, and it was an old telephone. I picked up the receiver but there was no answer. There's no recording and I never kept a copy of the program with my name on it, and no one alive remembers or cares that I played it in 1981, but there it was, a telephone on my white Formica kitchen table saying *I am the Barber Adagio you played in 1981, the string quartet version.*

The one in 1964 that Karajan conducted in Berlin was there too, and it was a plate of fine bone china. Next to it was the one, the very first one ever, that Toscanini conducted in 1938 in New York, and it was a Lamborghini. A 2009 one that Gustavo conducted in Mexico City was a postage stamp. Another said *I am the one conducted by Ozawa in 2019* and it was a coral reef. The one next to that was a bright light and it said *I am the Barber Adagio that you played in memory of your best friend Karl, who died from AIDS.*

Every Adagio for Strings in history was right there on my white Formica kitchen table, but time was running out—my cardiologist appointment was at noon. So, I left them laying there for all the world to hold, and headed out the door.

Beethoven Nine

After Matt Miller (while pondering the 200th anniversary of the first performance in Vienna)

We're just a couple of bars in
to the fourth movement, the crashing
tympani and brass, lower strings
entering in sagacious unison and
it hits me, a tsunami of dissonance,
here I am onstage in Carnegie,
I've got the hindquarters of a goat
and horns growing from my forehead,
but it's not Pan's flute I'm holding,
it's a violin, and I look around;
it seems we've lost our way,
primordial tones rise out of a mist,
staccato woodwinds dance with pagans,
pastoral longings are sung by a solo oboe
and that's the moment, the moment
I can't ever forget, seeing her face,
up there
in the chorus awaiting her entrance and,
I swear to the God, right there
on the stage, she transforms from
a mountain nymph to a pine spruce—
not even Beethoven could rescue her from
a hideous brute like me—
and as I raise the violin to my chin
I look down and see her face
inside my violin, inside
the curly maple and spruce,
emerald eyes gazing up at me,
voice vibrating,
Ode to Joy.

A Few Seconds of Joy

I want to give the world a few seconds of joy. That's my plan. Beethoven gave the world whole symphonies of joy, but I'm just trying to do my small part here, if no one minds.

I'm growing a Sitka spruce in my living room. Every day I tend to it, watering it with Debussy and fertilizing it with Mahler. I bring it with me to the hot practice room where it provides me with shade during long hours spent there. And at dusk it carries my bloodied and broken body to the pub.

Sometimes I climb high among the folded leaves, where a ray of sunlight is a platinum setting for tree rings. Their photographic memories store music married to light and their geometry adorns concert halls and caskets of kings and fools. It's no surprise that architects and acousticians choose trees: when the finale of Beethoven's Ninth comes to its resounding climax, it is the trees that get the last word.

I imagine some future architect choosing my Sitka spruce for its fine acoustic properties—cutting a handsome and wide-grained slab to be honed and carved, sanded and polished, becoming a proscenium of wood in a concert hall of the universe. One day, long after I'm gone, long after the last symphonies of Beethoven have evaporated, my fabulous tree will still be echoing a thousand billion seconds of joy.

I've Played a Lot of Broadway Shows in My Life,
Some of Them Huge Hits with Names Like
*Crazy for You, Fiddler on the Roof, Merrily We
Roll Along* (Once a Huge Flop, Later a Huge
Hit), and of Course the Ones That Never
Should Have Been Done in the First Place:
Carrie, Lestat, A Tale of Two Cities,

and there was this one called
Thou Shalt Not and the critics said

you shouldn't have written a show
about a guy thrown out of a boat and drowning

what makes you think
that tourists from Indiana and Kansas

arriving in New York the week after 9/11
will pay big bucks for parking and dinner

and then listen to songs
sung in a morgue?

that's like when you get up in the morning
and step on the bathroom scale

and it says you did this to yourself
another three and a half pounds

while a man you love
or a woman you wished you had loved

struggle in the night to get up off the kitchen floor
and you toss in your bed

the firehose of sweat
gushing from your pores trying to wash away

the black volcano atop your shoulders
the knife in your throat so sharp

there's something moving
down there inside of you

a snake that's writhing and snapping
enormous like the whale

struggling to get to the surface
before it suffocates

the audience is still up in the balcony
staring down with disbelieving eyes

gouged out and rolling onto the stage
and into the orchestra pit

but somewhere
just above you

a voice is singing
about love

about the one she loves
and he leans close to her

kisses her
on the bridge at Giverny

and I kid you not
Claude Monet is standing right there

putting it all on canvas
and that's the moment

the moment when
the blue haired lady in a wheelchair

from Wichita opens her purse
and writes a check

for dinner and a show
with some damn good tap

dance and song
and maybe a little rhythm of jazz to boot

Broadway Chocolate Pushers

Every Broadway pit orchestra has at least one chocolate pusher.
At *Book of Mormon* they go with 92%, but at *Wicked* they are hardcore
100% Cocoa junkies. At *The Music Man,* Hugh Jackman was Harold Hill
and a violinist brought her son's Wolverine lunch box full of candy
into the pit. Somewhere between Trouble and Shipoopi
it got passed around for chili flavored chocolate
spicy red hots to munch on during the off beats.

Anything to get the band through
the 432nd performance of *Les Mis*
before the violinist's arms fall off
or the trumpet player is left hanging from his lips
atop the barricade on the Rue Plumet.
Most of the time it's dark chocolate,
but some pits fancy gummy worms
like we had at *Follies*. I avoided the sour notes
but there was Lindt. The more the better,
more sweetness—what could be sweeter than
better Broadway through sugar?

The night we cranked out *Into the Woods*
number 500 with jellybeans on our music stands
the audience had tears coming down during *No One Is Alone,*
but then Bernadette Peters came out and sang *Children Will Listen.*

That was the moment when the giants dropped like Milk Duds
out of the sky. They melted under the spotlights
and into the orchestra pit where the last violist was mixing
the saltiness of sweat with the sweetness of a truffle
as his two-year-old daughter waited
for her Dad to come home
with the Milky Way under her tongue.

I Am Not a Violin

Nothing unreal exists and yet
I lie in pieces:
spruce, maple, rosewood, cuttings of ebony.
Alongside fine chisels and sandpaper, I wait

for the artisan's glue so that I may rise again
and wander the world to protect you.
Like air, I'll rise.
I am your canopy of trees.

Coltrane took his sax out of the case
and made it look easy.
With butterflies and ravens
his fingers flew

rising like moons and suns—
the Coltrane riffs, they kept
bending the blues, waggling the improv
with the certainty of tides,

the alto, the tenor, the real, the unreal
existing in pieces, in riffs
made up. I never could make shit up
but still, I fly. I am your compass—

I am not a violin, I am not a sax,
more an orphan sold by nuns
to Sephardic Jews. They glued me together
and sent me out to wander the world.

About the Author

Martin Agee's career as a violinist has brought him to the major concert venues, recording studios and theatres of New York City for over thirty-five years. His television, recording and performing credits include more than forty original Broadway cast albums, and encompass a wide array of concert performances with the major artists of our time from Itzhak Perlman to Yannick Nézet-Séguin, and from Madonna to Metallica. In January 2020, Points of Light, the world's foremost organization dedicated to the promotion and fostering of volunteerism, awarded Martin Agee the Daily Point of Light Award. *Not a Violin* is his first full-length poetry collection.

www.ingramcontent.com/pod-product-compliance
Lightning Source LLC
Chambersburg PA
CBHW070936160426
43193CB00011B/1702